JESUS KNOWS YOUR NAME

Walking in the Presence of God

CHRISTOPHER CALEB

Christopher Caleb @ 2020 - All rights reserved.

This book is written with the sole purpose of providing relevant information on a specific topic for which every effort has been made to ensure that it is both accurate and reasonable. Nevertheless, by purchasing this eBook you consent to the fact that the author, as well as the publisher, are in no way experts on the topics contained herein, regardless of any claims as such that may be made within.

The content of this book is not intended for proselytism or religious propaganda but is the result of the author's thought.

No part of this publication may be reproduced, stored in a retrieval system, or transmitted in any form or by any means — electronic, mechanical, photocopy, recording, or any other — except for brief quotations in printed reviews, without the prior permission of the publisher.

Scripture quotations are taken from the World English Bible (WEB) in Public Domain and belong to eBible.org.

≈ TABLE OF CONTENTS ≈

INTRODUCTION 7

PART I - FOLLOWING THE LORD IN SILENCE 11
CHAPTER 1 - THE TRUE ADORATION 13
CHAPTER 2 – THE JOB'S SILENCE 17
CHAPTER 3 - JESUS ANOINTED AT BETHANY 21
CHAPTER 4 - IN THE SYNAGOGUE OF NAZARETH 25
CHAPTER 5 - THE ADULTEROUS WOMAN 27
CHAPTER 6 – JESUS BEFORE HEROD 31
CHAPTER 7 – THE TRANSFIGURATION 33
CHAPTER 8 – MARTHA AND MARY 37
CHAPTER 9 - JESUS AND THE MIRACULOUS CATCH OF FISH 39
CHAPTER 10 - OPENING OF THE SEVENTH SEAL 43
CHAPTER 11 - THE LAMB AND ITS REDEEMED ON MOUNT SION 47
CHAPTER 12 – THE NEW JERUSALEM 51

PART II - TO THIS YOU WERE CALLED 53
CHAPTER 13 - NEW CLOTHES 55
CHAPTER 14 - GUIDE FOR THE BLIND 65
CHAPTER 15 - THE CHURCH DESTINED FOR THE KINGDOM 69
CHAPTER 16 - MEETING WITH THE KING 79
CHAPTER 17 - THE MEETING AT THE SEA OF TIBERIAS (*in-depth study*) 87

CONCLUSION 97

"...but rejoice that your names are written in heaven"

Luke 10: 20

INTRODUCTION

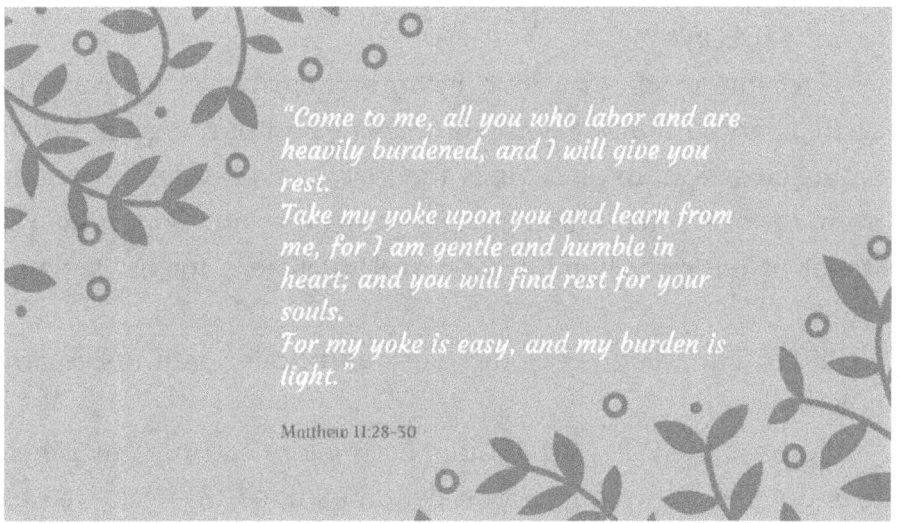

"Come to me, all you who labor and are heavily burdened, and I will give you rest.
Take my yoke upon you and learn from me, for I am gentle and humble in heart; and you will find rest for your souls.
For my yoke is easy, and my burden is light."

Matthew 11:28-30

Jesus' invitation is clear. It is addressed to the troubled and aggravated, not to others. To those who think that their burden is too great and that there are no solutions, and perhaps they turn to others in the hope of being helped or "lightened": Jesus' invitation is addressed to them.

He, with a sweet voice full of power, gives the solution: "Come to Me". Only He can understand, only He can console, only He can free, because every podesta has been given to Him by the Father.

He, Jesus, is the true rest.

Some present religions, others present their work, and still, others use Scripture to convince, but all this serves no purpose. Only one can solve every problem, whether big or small: His name is JESUS!

He, loving us with love incomprehensible to us, came to earth, charged himself with all our sins and burdens, and died on the cross for our sins. He is the Just One; in order to save us from certain condemnation, He overcame sin, and now He stands at the right hand of God and intercedes for us day and night.

So to Him alone goes the glory and honor, and not to any other.

Jesus is the Way, the Truth, and the Life and not any other. It is not the various religious denominations that can free us from our sins and problems; it is not even the verses learned by heart or recited in scripture that can save us, but only the Lord Jesus. The invitation is to the needy, and not to those who feel righteous, and have no (as they say) need of anything because they now belong to some denomination.

Know man that only through Jesus do we go to the Father, and not by other means!

Great is the love of God who gave us Jesus the Lord, and He ascended to the Father. He did not leave us alone but sent us the Holy Spirit to guide us in every truth. Today many have replaced the guidance and anointing of the Holy Spirit with literal knowledge of Scripture.

But the only one can present Jesus, only one can speak of Him, and only one can make us feel His presence: *the Holy Spirit*!

God, who has all of creation at his command, is pleased to use man, so he must recognize that he is nothing and nothing can he do by himself, and therefore must give all the glory and praise to the Lord Jesus.

Like Jesus, when He came to this earth, He obeyed the Father in everything from the cradle to the cross, and never used His earthly ministry for His glory; so, His servants do nothing to attract any glory to themselves, but point to and present only one: Jesus the King and the Lord of our life; and after they have accomplished all things commanded by Him they hide in Christ, so that souls may remain with Jesus.

Thus also, we desire to present the King Jesus and remain hidden in Him. This is also the desire of His Church, which has no denominations, but is formed by "true worshippers, who worship God in spirit and truth"; this Church is "Invisible" and not known by man, but is known by the Lord Jesus.

PART I - FOLLOWING THE LORD IN SILENCE

CHAPTER 1 - THE TRUE ADORATION

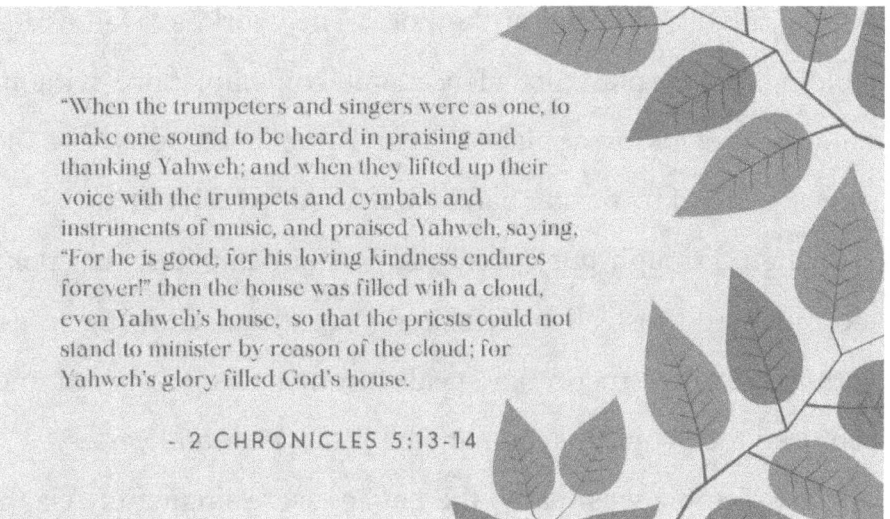

"When the trumpeters and singers were as one, to make one sound to be heard in praising and thanking Yahweh; and when they lifted up their voice with the trumpets and cymbals and instruments of music, and praised Yahweh, saying, "For he is good, for his loving kindness endures forever!" then the house was filled with a cloud, even Yahweh's house, so that the priests could not stand to minister by reason of the cloud; for Yahweh's glory filled God's house."

- 2 CHRONICLES 5:13-14

The stones, before being used for building, were worked in the quarry with hammer, ax and other instruments, and everyone could hear all sorts of noise that very often, in the passer-by's ear, was annoying, and some even complained.

Sometimes this leads us to think that even "zealous" souls prefer a language that contains only noise, to that anointed by the Holy Spirit.

Today in churches this is what is happening: instead of being consoled and blessed, we hear only noises, brouhahas, and cries that distract us from the glorious vision of Jesus

Christ. The time will come when every chosen one, if he or she lets himself or herself be worked by the Holy Spirit, will become a stone for the building of the Lord. This work, as well as the building, takes place in silence and contemplation, without clamors, crowds or applause. Many, in silence, saw how the stones, worked by master hands, were tied to each other.

Often, through our solicitude, and our impetus, we spoke too much and instead of remaining silent and allowing Jesus, with His infinite mercy, to speak to our souls, we bored and confused the people, using many biblical words and verses.

The Temple was ready, the Levites were singing of Asaph, Heman, Jeduthun, and the priests were playing and singing praises to the Lord, as the House was filled with the Lord's cloud, and He took the presidency.

The cloud is the figure of the guide and the Holy Spirit. Indeed, the Lord guided the people in the desert with a cloud during the day: when it stopped or moved again, the people had to do the same. This leads to an absolute dependence on the Holy Spirit, and blessed are we, if we are in this condition! In the temple, there were no more sounds or songs; the cloud had invaded the House, silence had been established because God took the presidency.

God was present, and the priests could no longer stay; there was no more noise, and no more exaggerated cults. The man disappeared and entered into true adoration!

CHAPTER 2 – THE JOB'S SILENCE

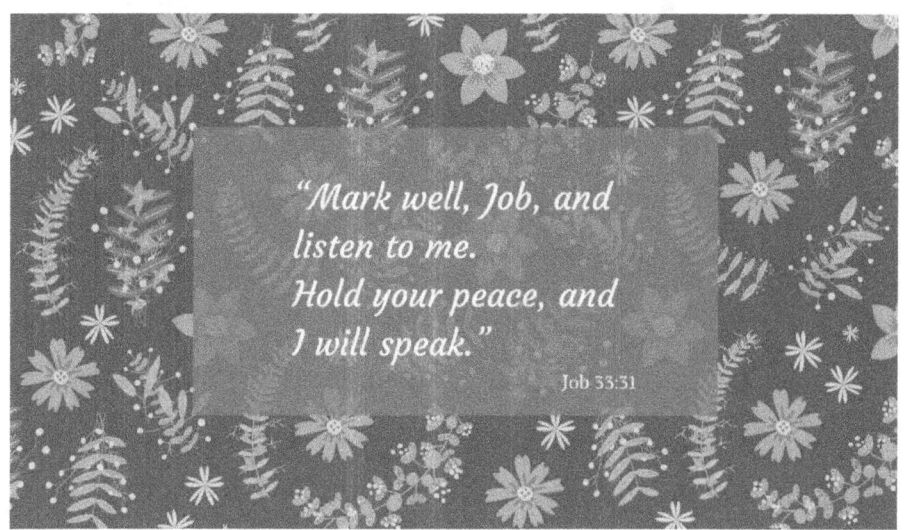

Job's friends, as a result of his suffering, went to visit him at home; they thought that what had happened to Job was a misfortune. But the Holy Spirit reveals to us that the many sufferings led Job to lose himself and to seek the Lord.

It is not given to everyone to follow the Lord in silence; far from us to judge others. We must come by grace to renounce ourselves, take up the cross and serve Jesus to become His disciples. It is precisely the sufferings that lead us to see, hear and know Him; elevating us to a greater stature in the Kingdom of the Spirit. Let us thank God for the suffering!

Although the friends had talked so much, they had not achieved anything because Job justified himself. Today many people justify themselves, but only One can justify man: Jesus Christ.

Among the three, there was a moment of silence, but Someone spoke to man internally, He who patiently waited for the man to be silent.

Today many bother the soul with so many words, but only One is He who can speak and restore souls. Elihu, a figure of Jesus Christ, waited for everyone to speak and then said: "Be silent and I will teach you wisdom".

Man, before teaching, is invited to listen. There isn't teaching if the man is not willing to listen. Many times God uses a servant who is not appreciated by religious crowds, and when he speaks, he is not listened to because no souls are willing to do so, and because they look only at the visible. It is precisely among the despised that Jesus moves because He was despised by the religious officers of Jerusalem.

Job, though silent, reasoned, and there was a stern but gentle warning from Elihu: "Wait, O Job, hear me; be silent, and I will speak".

Souls in churches are very solicitous in speaking, but the warning is to wait for God to speak from heaven, a warning that led Job to understand that He who spoke was a messenger from heaven.

Shut up, stop justifying yourself and entrust yourself to Him who justified the world!

God loved Job, who was brought face to face with Him, not in front men, who flatter souls.

Job had to exclaim further on, "I had heard of Thee, but my eye saw Thee".

It is one thing to hear about Jesus, it is another to see Him. To see Him, we must remain silent: it's in this condition that He acts.

When the disciples were behind closed doors, locked, in silence, careful not to make noise because the Jews could hear and go to fetch them, in that silence of fear, Jesus entered and said: "Peace be with you". Only He knows how to intervene at opportune moments and speak.

When Job was silent, the Lord began to speak. Samuel said, "Speak, Lord, that your servant hears you," can we say the same?

CHAPTER 3 - JESUS ANOINTED AT BETHANY

"Then, six days before the Passover, Jesus came to Bethany, where Lazarus was, who had been dead, whom he raised from the dead. So they made him a supper there. Martha served, but Lazarus was one of those who sat at the table with him. Therefore Mary took a pound of ointment of pure nard, very precious, and anointed Jesus's feet and wiped his feet with her hair. The house was filled with the fragrance of the ointment.

Then Judas Iscariot, Simon's son, one of his disciples, who would betray him, said, "Why wasn't this ointment sold for three hundred denarii and given to the poor?" Now he said this, not because he cared for the poor, but because he was a thief, and having the money box, used to steal what was put into it. But Jesus said, "Leave her alone. She has kept this for the day of my burial. For you always have the poor with you, but you don't always have me."

A large crowd therefore of the Jews learned that he was there; and they came, not for Jesus' sake only, but that they might see Lazarus also, whom he had raised from the dead. But the chief priests conspired to put Lazarus to death also because on account of him many of the Jews went away and believed in Jesus."

John 12: 1-11

At the banquet in Bethany, a glorious event was celebrated: the resurrection of Lazarus; many people went to the banquet and Martha ministered to them.

They that are disciplined by heaven await the time when the Son of man shall take his place at the feast, as the Shulammite did, saying: "While the king is in my feast, my nard hath made his smell". First, the King takes the chair, and then the spikenard makes the smell.

At Bethany's feast, all eyes are on Him. He is always present, but we often show indifference to Him. Jesus manifests Himself in His servants and enters some banquet, but He is often overlooked because other masters have taken the place of the true Master.

Those who have been disciplined in the school of Jesus Christ are not looking for false masters, but are only attracted to Him who created and formed them, just as it was for Mary and her church of which she is a daughter.

She did not neglect Jesus and was not attracted to the festivities or those around her, but she turned directly to Him, threw herself at His feet, and began to anoint them, and drying them with Her hair.

Between the church and Jesus, there is no noise; communication takes place in the spirit, as Jesus also speaks through silence.

While the woman was anointing the Lord's feet, there was a strange talk in the hall.

In every place where Jesus is anointed, we will hear this talk.

Today, while people look for crowds, honors, personal glory and neglect Him who is worthy of honor and glory, the Lord's delight escapes all this and is present only when in spirit He is called as the Lord.

The time has come when all those who wish to serve the Lord must be ready to live a life hidden in Christ, far from the hullabaloo, and the rackets that last for a time. This was what Mary had understood, and had chosen what lasts for eternity.

In that room, there was a scent of holiness and so it is between Jesus and His bride!

Zacchaeus had the desire to invite Jesus to his house and He said to him: "Today I come to your house.

Zacchaeus was willing to receive Jesus in his house and He went and worked in his life, bringing health into his house. Later Zacchaeus gave half of his goods to the poor and paid those he had defrauded up to four fold.

It is not enough to call oneself God's child, but one must renounce oneself and serve Jesus.

He said: "Not he who says Lord will enter the Kingdom of Heaven, but he who does the will of My Father". It is vain to celebrate cults where He is not honored.

In His presence, we must present ourselves with broken hearts, we must anoint Him, dry Him with our hair, kiss those wounds that have been opened because of us, and stand at His feet and be ready to be taught. His teachings cancel our attitudes, our goals, our ambitions, and make us understand that we have been called by grace to *follow in His footsteps in silence*!

In witnessing that scene between Mary and Jesus, the others were amazed. Even the angels learn from the church the varied wisdom of God!

CHAPTER 4 - IN THE SYNAGOGUE OF NAZARETH

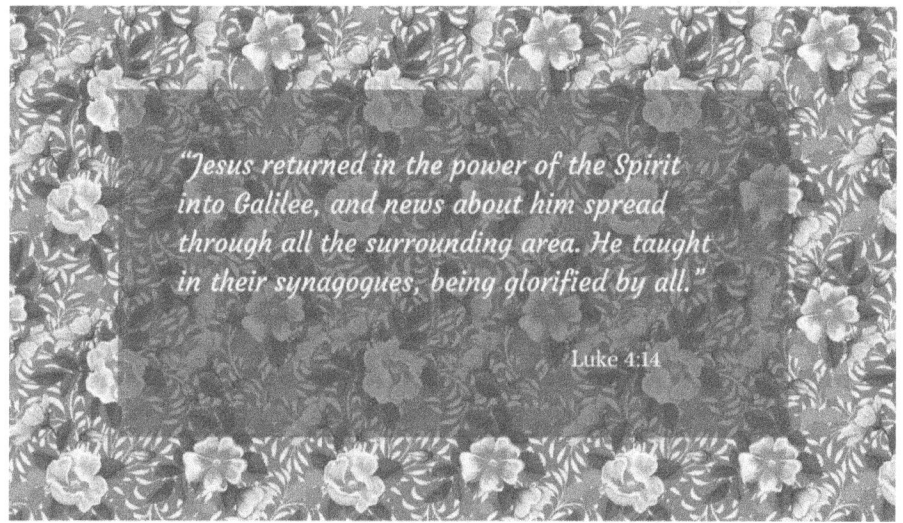

"Jesus returned in the power of the Spirit into Galilee, and news about him spread through all the surrounding area. He taught in their synagogues, being glorified by all."

Luke 4:14

God has granted us Jesus as the Master for our souls, and we silently have to learn at His school. Although He was the incarnate wisdom, for many years, Jesus went every Saturday to the synagogue to hear "masters" who so often trained outside of God's will; yet Jesus listened and did not stop them until the day came when He was commanded from on High, and He stood up and read.

Only by remaining in His school do we become true disciples, because it is He who calls us and forms us, and so we can listen and follow the true Master.

Jesus' years of silence must be of great instruction for us. In this time, there are many "masters" who have taken the place of the Master. We often happened to hear sermons read from the Bible and then interpreted with false discernment, confusing the souls in the various places of worship. All this, because we want to act for ourselves and not wait for the Holy Spirit to speak to our souls.

Who knows how many times even our Lord Jesus shuddered in the Spirit ,but He, in silence, and in obedience, Saturday after Saturday, waited for the moment commanded by the Father.

We too, before we decide to abandon a church where there is a strange master, we must wait in silence and obedience for the command that comes from on High.

We often leave churches hurriedly, without command, because we have no patience to wait.

When Jesus left the temple, he did not comment, he did not argue about the wrong teachings, but said, "This is no longer the house of my Father". We too are called not to comment, to remain where God has put us, in silence, in suffering, praying that on a blessed day, the command to rise will come, as it came to Joshua.

At that moment, the servant will rise and exclaim: "I stretch myself beyond, because I am thirsty for Jesus!"

CHAPTER 5 - THE ADULTEROUS WOMAN

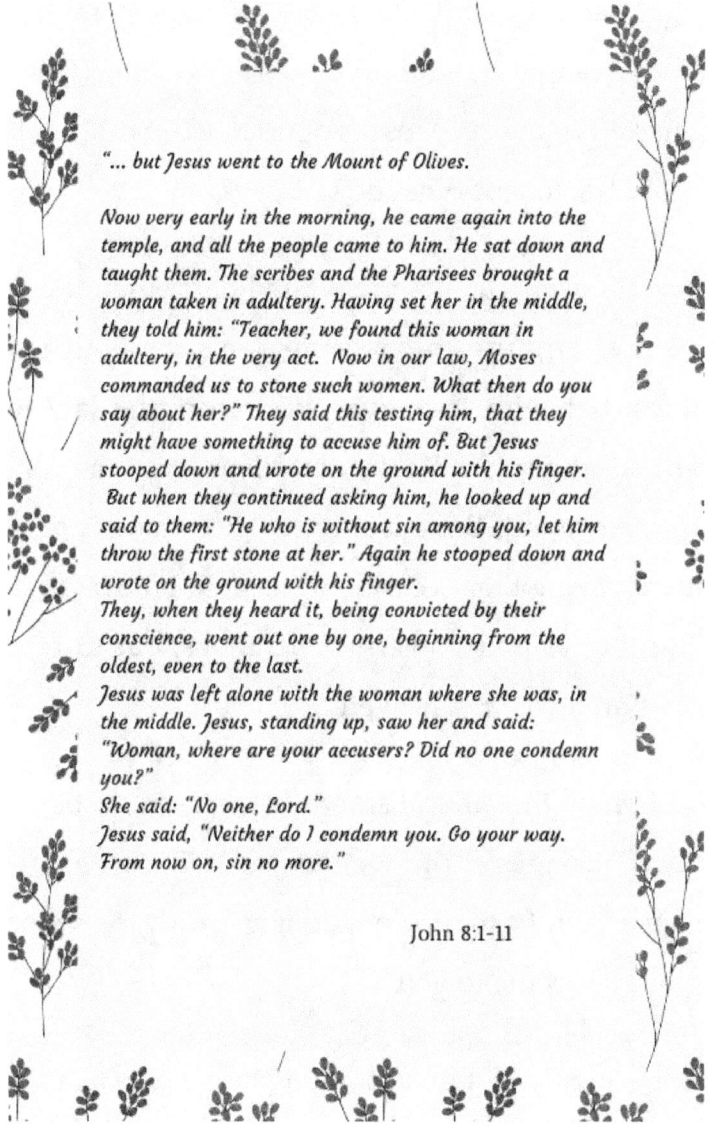

"... but Jesus went to the Mount of Olives.

Now very early in the morning, he came again into the temple, and all the people came to him. He sat down and taught them. The scribes and the Pharisees brought a woman taken in adultery. Having set her in the middle, they told him: "Teacher, we found this woman in adultery, in the very act. Now in our law, Moses commanded us to stone such women. What then do you say about her?" They said this testing him, that they might have something to accuse him of. But Jesus stooped down and wrote on the ground with his finger. But when they continued asking him, he looked up and said to them: "He who is without sin among you, let him throw the first stone at her." Again he stooped down and wrote on the ground with his finger.
They, when they heard it, being convicted by their conscience, went out one by one, beginning from the oldest, even to the last.
Jesus was left alone with the woman where she was, in the middle. Jesus, standing up, saw her and said: "Woman, where are your accusers? Did no one condemn you?"
She said: "No one, Lord."
Jesus said, "Neither do I condemn you. Go your way. From now on, sin no more."

John 8:1-11

While Jesus was teaching in the temple, some scribes and Pharisees brought him a woman caught in adultery and said to him, "This woman has committed adultery, Moses commanded us in the law that these should be stoned, What do you say?"

Today, there are many scribes and Pharisees in the churches who also use scripture to condemn souls who fall into some temptations; but with Jesus, we went from the law to grace. Jesus kept *silent* and while He was silent, with one finger, He wrote on the ground; there is a time when things are not said, but written. On another occasion, Jesus told His disciples not to rejoice in miracles and powerful operations, but to rejoice that their names are *written* in heaven.

We all know the biblical story; the accusers went away and Jesus did not condemn the woman but said to her: "I do not condemn you, but from now on, do not sin any more; today, the day of grace has come to you".

This is a moment of great training; let us also learn *in silence* to pardon the unfortunate, not forgetting that the Lord has given us teachings, to love our enemies; let us learn not to be solicitous in judging our neighbor, because judgment belongs to the Lord.

While man condemns, God absolves.

Who knows how many times we too have been among the accusers, but the day has come that at His school, we learn to know human misery, and now the world awaits the manifestation of God's children. Jesus is the restorer of all ruins, He has come to save what was lost.

We must become trees of coolness and shelter for everyone and understand that the Lord is merciful.

CHAPTER 6 – JESUS BEFORE HEROD

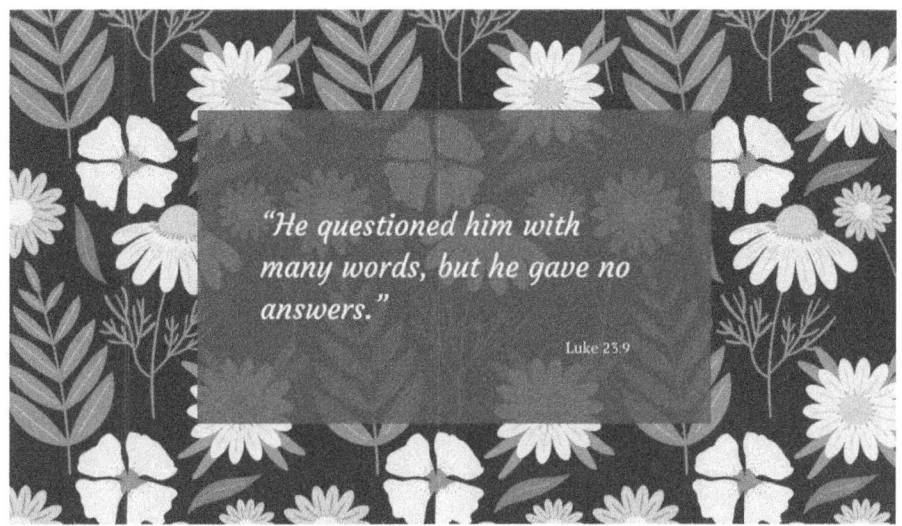

"He questioned him with many words, but he gave no answers."

Luke 23:9

Jesus was brought before Herod, who began to ask Him many questions, but He did not answer.

People ask many questions to satisfy their curiosity; many wish to see signs, miracles, wonders out of pure curiosity and Herod was one of them. The Holy Spirit leads us to see the face of Jesus filled with mercy, always ready to forgive, but never to satisfy human curiosity. He teaches us to seek the Kingdom of God. Instead of being willing to receive Jesus, people are interested in the visible, the crowds, the enthusiasms and the miracles.

Herod's curiosity was not satisfied; let us pray to God that we too may have the same Spirit as Jesus, not satisfying human curiosity, *keeping silent* and not giving what is Holy to dogs, but speaking only by command of the Holy Spirit.

CHAPTER 7 – THE TRANSFIGURATION

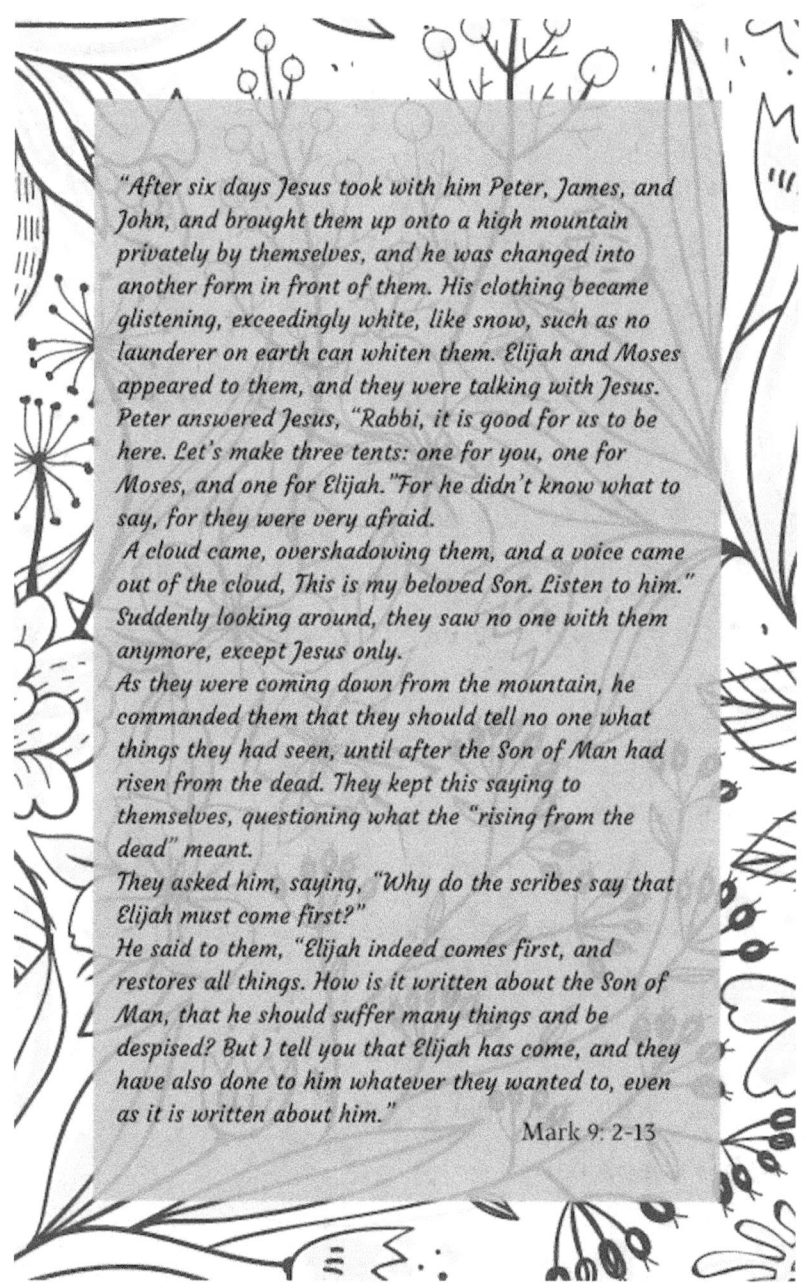

"After six days Jesus took with him Peter, James, and John, and brought them up onto a high mountain privately by themselves, and he was changed into another form in front of them. His clothing became glistening, exceedingly white, like snow, such as no launderer on earth can whiten them. Elijah and Moses appeared to them, and they were talking with Jesus. Peter answered Jesus, "Rabbi, it is good for us to be here. Let's make three tents: one for you, one for Moses, and one for Elijah." For he didn't know what to say, for they were very afraid.

A cloud came, overshadowing them, and a voice came out of the cloud, This is my beloved Son. Listen to him." Suddenly looking around, they saw no one with them anymore, except Jesus only.

As they were coming down from the mountain, he commanded them that they should tell no one what things they had seen, until after the Son of Man had risen from the dead. They kept this saying to themselves, questioning what the "rising from the dead" meant.

They asked him, saying, "Why do the scribes say that Elijah must come first?"

He said to them, "Elijah indeed comes first, and restores all things. How is it written about the Son of Man, that he should suffer many things and be despised? But I tell you that Elijah has come, and they have also done to him whatever they wanted to, even as it is written about him."

Mark 9: 2-13

Jesus invited Peter, James and John to follow Him on a high mountain, and they did so *in silence*.

The important thing is never to lose His vision even if you have to face many difficulties. It often happens that we lose sight of Him, dwelling on vain reasoning, and losing His vision.

Jesus will give us the strength to overcome every obstacle if we desire to follow in His footsteps and silently do His will.

Following the Lord in silence costs sacrifice; the same was for the disciples who arrived at the top of the mountain and were rewarded: they saw Jesus as they had never seen Him before, all blazing.

At a certain point, Elijah and Moses appeared and the disciples were brought to a high revelation.

Blessed are we if we are made to work by the Lord to acquire new revelations and lose everything that does not please Him, and is only valid for a time.

Despite the glorious revelation, Peter wanted to keep Elijah and Moses with them. We too often want to hold back what the Lord has not prepared.

The disciples were amazed when a cloud came to them, and from it came a voice that said, "This is my beloved Son; listen to Him," and at that instant, only Jesus remained.

Many things must disappear from our lives, even if they may seem good, but can prevent the complete revelation of Jesus.

The disciples came down from the mountain with Him with a new revelation.

When He calls us, He does so for greater revelation and we *silently*, without question, must follow Him to contemplate His glory.

CHAPTER 8 – MARTHA AND MARY

> *As they went on their way, he entered into a certain village, and a certain woman named Martha received him into her house. She had a sister called Mary, who also sat at Jesus' feet and heard his word. But Martha was distracted with much serving, and she came up to him, and said, "Lord, don't you care that my sister left me to serve alone? Ask her therefore to help me."*
> *Jesus answered her, "Martha, Martha, you are anxious and troubled about many things, but one thing is needed. Mary has chosen the good part, which will not be taken away from her."*
>
> Luke 10: 38-42

Jesus entered Martha and Mary's house, who stood before the King of Glory; His face shone more than the sun, and grace was scattered on His lips.

When He comes, He gives peace, serenity, and tranquillity; let us contemplate Him through the Holy Spirit! He is in our house, He knows that we need Him, but many times, despite His arrival, we neglect Him because we are caught up in so many thoughts, noises and interests. In His infinite mercy, Jesus waits for us to get tired of ourselves, and *in silence,* He embraces us and takes us into His rest.

Martha was straining around what is vain, while Mary was at the King's feet. The Lord said: "*Unless Yahweh builds the house, they who build it labor in vain.*"(Psalm 127:1)

Only what the Holy Spirit does is eternal and Mary knew this well, for she left all that she was doing and sat *in silence* at Jesus' feet.

She understood that Jesus desired communion, so she contemplated Him and listened to Him speak while Martha turned to Jesus saying: "Lord my sister has left me alone to serve you, tell her to help me", but Mary *silently* continued to listen to Him, choosing the best part.

Today, we too are too busy and worried about ourselves; let us pray to the Lord that He will purge us with the Holy Spirit and with fire from all that is in vain, to enter into communion with Him!

CHAPTER 9 - JESUS AND THE MIRACULOUS CATCH OF FISH

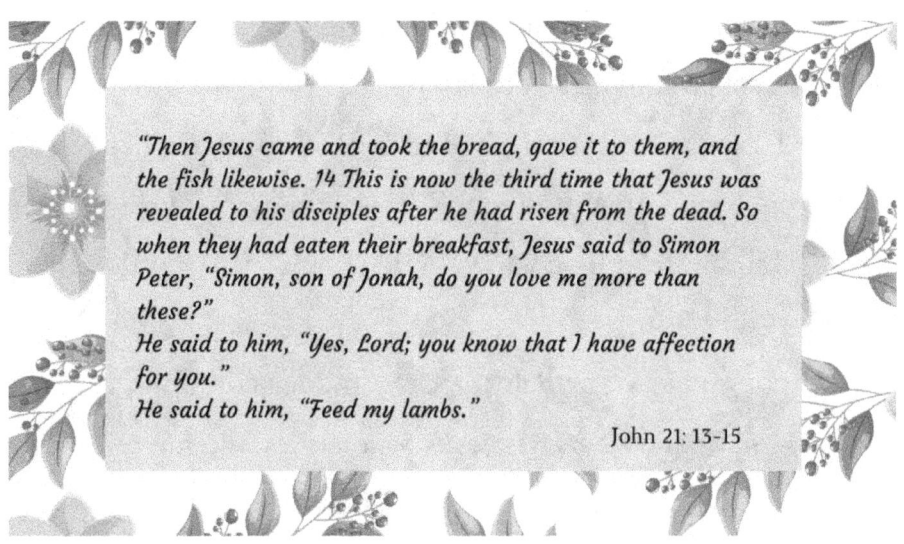

"Then Jesus came and took the bread, gave it to them, and the fish likewise. 14 This is now the third time that Jesus was revealed to his disciples after he had risen from the dead. So when they had eaten their breakfast, Jesus said to Simon Peter, "Simon, son of Jonah, do you love me more than these?"
He said to him, "Yes, Lord; you know that I have affection for you."
He said to him, "Feed my lambs."

John 21: 13-15

Jesus appeared near the Sea of Tiberias.

In the life of the resurrection, the bride is prepared by the Holy Spirit. That's why the disciples saw roasted fish and bread on the shore of the burning embers,.

Everything that comes down from heaven cannot be boiled, but is roasted with *fire*; boiled food is presented by man, but for those who love Jesus, this food is indigestible.

The bride desires true food, the food that does not flatter, that does not fascinate, that is not for a time, but desires the reality; and this is presented only by the Holy Spirit.

Jesus asked Peter, "Do you love me?" Peter answered yes, but Jesus asked him three times.

God knows everything about us, He has known us since before the foundation of the world; for Him, we are many open books, but unfortunately, we still know very little about ourselves and Jesus.

Although He knew Peter's heart, and asked him if he loved him, this happened because Jesus wanted a dialogue with him; he wanted to lead him to new revelations.

Jesus prepared profound revelations for us, but we are closed in ourselves, we often cannot receive them. The Lord knew the name of Jacob, but despite this, he wanted to know it from him, so that Jacob could receive more revelations; the Lord said to him, "You will no longer be called Jacob, but Israel," that is, Prince of the Lord.

Only He can lead us to greater revelations, and He can make us understand that the path cannot be faced with human forces, but with those of God; for nothing unclean will enter the Kingdom of the Spirit.

Jesus led Peter to a greater revelation and said to him: "When you were young (not yet mature) you would gird yourself and go where you wanted, but when you are old (a mature saint) you will stretch out your hands and another will gird you and lead you where you do not want to go".

For a time we too have walked a lot; we have made decisions that we believed were right, but today is another time when we must act only at the Lord's command, obeying Jesus alone, doing His will and *silently following in His footsteps.*

Later Jesus said to Peter: "Follow me." Peter, instead of obeying His command turned around and saw that John also followed Jesus.

Unlike Peter, John, who received the same command in the Spirit, obeyed in silence, without distraction and without meddling in what was happening around him.

We must learn this; living at Jesus' feet, we must do what He commands us without turning back, but looking straight to our Luminary, King of Glory.

The prophet Ezekiel saw cherubims, a figure of the church, who walked straight ahead wherever the Holy Spirit guided them, without looking back either way.

We too, like Peter, although we have the command to follow Jesus, still look at too many things and do not realize that there are true servants of the Lord who are into Spirit and silence, and have consecrated themselves to Him; following Him, just as John did.

Jesus had to answer Peter with love: "What is that to you? *Follow me*"!

CHAPTER 10 - OPENING OF THE SEVENTH SEAL

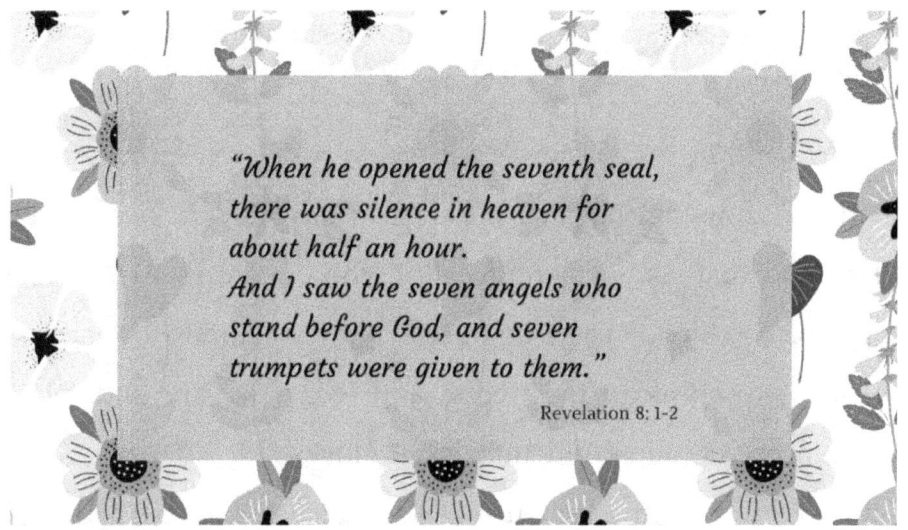

"When he opened the seventh seal, there was silence in heaven for about half an hour.
And I saw the seven angels who stand before God, and seven trumpets were given to them."

Revelation 8: 1-2

A half-hour of silence was observed in heaven; time is in God's hands and is not measured according to the measure of the man.

To understand this, many seals must be dissolved in our lives, and this is a work that only the Lord can do.

In the construction of the temple, the stones were worked and cut in the quarry, this operation involved a lot of noise from hammer and chisel, but when they were brought to the surface, to the light and placed next to each other by master hands, these noises ceased and a temple to the praise of God was built.

The difficultly is to abandon oneself *silently* into God's hands and to be placed where He has established; only in this case, will we begin to experience true spiritual growth.

We still act as masters, as if we were the masters of souls, without knowing that many things in our life still need to be done and that souls belong to Him who bought them with the price of His blood. The true Master knows the most opportune moment to speak to the weary, and we, if we are under His guidance, can be instruments for His glory.

This is the time when our life must enter into a divine silence, admiring and contemplating Jesus.

We had the time to make noises, to raise a lot of dust, and to do religious propaganda, but there is still a lot left in the quarry: it is now the time to give space to the Master Hands to work and bring everything to light so that we become living stones for the building of God's temple.

The Lord's work in us is glorious.

Psalm 45 speaks about the bride of the Lord, and says: "I recite my works to the King", we still have much to say, but the time will come when by the Holy Spirit, we will begin to see the beauty of our Bridegroom Jesus and begin to be drawn to Him; stop talking and enter into a holy silence.

Just when we enter into this spiritual dimension and hear His voice saying: "Forget your people, and your father's house, and the King will give love to your beauty;" we will receive more revelations and He will fill us with His glory.

Philip spoke of Jesus to Nathanael, not presenting himself or his wisdom, but Jesus.

A few words: "Come and see" and we put into practice the half-hour of silence that was done in heaven; we begin to see in our lives the work that the Lord Jesus did and we allow souls to hear what holy things come from heaven.

CHAPTER 11 - THE LAMB AND ITS REDEEMED ON MOUNT SION

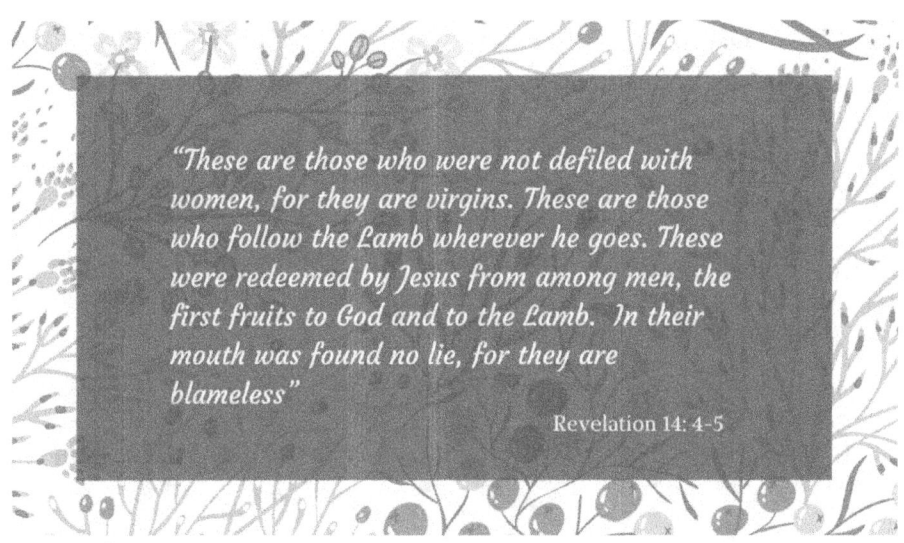

"These are those who were not defiled with women, for they are virgins. These are those who follow the Lamb wherever he goes. These were redeemed by Jesus from among men, the first fruits to God and to the Lamb. In their mouth was found no lie, for they are blameless"

Revelation 14: 4-5

God has brought us to an important spiritual stature, we are at the mount of Zion, the mount of God's holiness.

In the book of the Acts of the Apostles, it is written that for many sufferings, we will enter the Kingdom of God. Being elected costs; it is necessary to accept the plan that God has prepared for each of us.

The cost comes from the fact that we often love our reputation more than Jesus Christ, but to become Christ's bride, we have to renounce ourselves: we have to be ground up, incinerated.

The Holy Spirit has led us to this spiritual stature, without so much clamor, to look no longer at ourselves and those around us, but only at the Lamb of God.

The one hundred and forty-four thousand prophetic number are first fruits to God; they follow the Luminary wherever He goes.

For these, the time to follow men, religions or to rely on themselves has ended, but the time has begun in which one will walk, following reality, the one's own Master: Jesus the King of glory.

For a long time we have followed many people, and many emotions; we have gone to many places, but now we find ourselves before another time, which is to move only at the command of the Lord. Even alone, not understood, and victimized, but with Jesus. The difficult thing is not to move, but to be firm, lucid, and attentive to the Lord's command. Esau brought with him four hundred horsemen, they ran and made much dust; he invited Jacob to proceed with him at his own pace, but Jacob, who is a prince of the Lord and who had another vision, said to his brother, "You go, I will continue at the step of the sheep". With Jesus before us, we are drawn to

Him and *in silence* we follow Him wherever He goes, standing still when He commands us to stand still.

CHAPTER 12 – THE NEW JERUSALEM

> "There will be no curse any more. The throne of God and of the Lamb will be in it, and his servants will serve him.
> They will see his face, and his name will be on their foreheads. There will be no night, and they need no lamp light or sunlight; for the Lord God will illuminate them. They will reign forever and ever."
>
> Revelation 22: 3-5

A half-hour of *silence* was made in heaven and we learned that half of our life must be spent contemplating Jesus to enter into true service. His servants will serve Him and see His face.

Moses desired to see the Lord, but He said to him, "You will see me from behind," and so it happened, yet His face was changed: it shone so brightly that it had to wear a veil to speak with others.

At this spiritual stature, we no longer see Jesus from behind, but face to face; there are no more veils that separate us from Him and obscure our vision.

Paul said that the Church appeared in front of Jesus, glorious.

For the elect, the time of agitation is over because the name of God is written on their foreheads. They have passed from emotions to reality: Jesus is the reality.

In the past, we have served ourselves and men more than the Lord. Now, in following Jesus *in silence* and seeing Him face to face, we have entered into true service; we walk with His vision and finally, everything that prevented us from serving Him as He wants, has fallen.

The other luminaries have disappeared because Jesus enlightens us and leads us into the splendor of His glory.

True worshippers worship and serve the Lord in Spirit and truth; no longer false worshippers, who seek Jesus only for their own material interests and for the crowds, but true worshippers who desire Jesus because He is their only purpose in life. They are in love with Him and feel privileged to silently serve the King in His beauty. Amen.

PART II - TO THIS YOU WERE CALLED

*"For you were called to this,
because Christ also suffered for us,
leaving you an example,
that you should follow his steps"*

1 Peter 2: 21

CHAPTER 13 - NEW CLOTHES

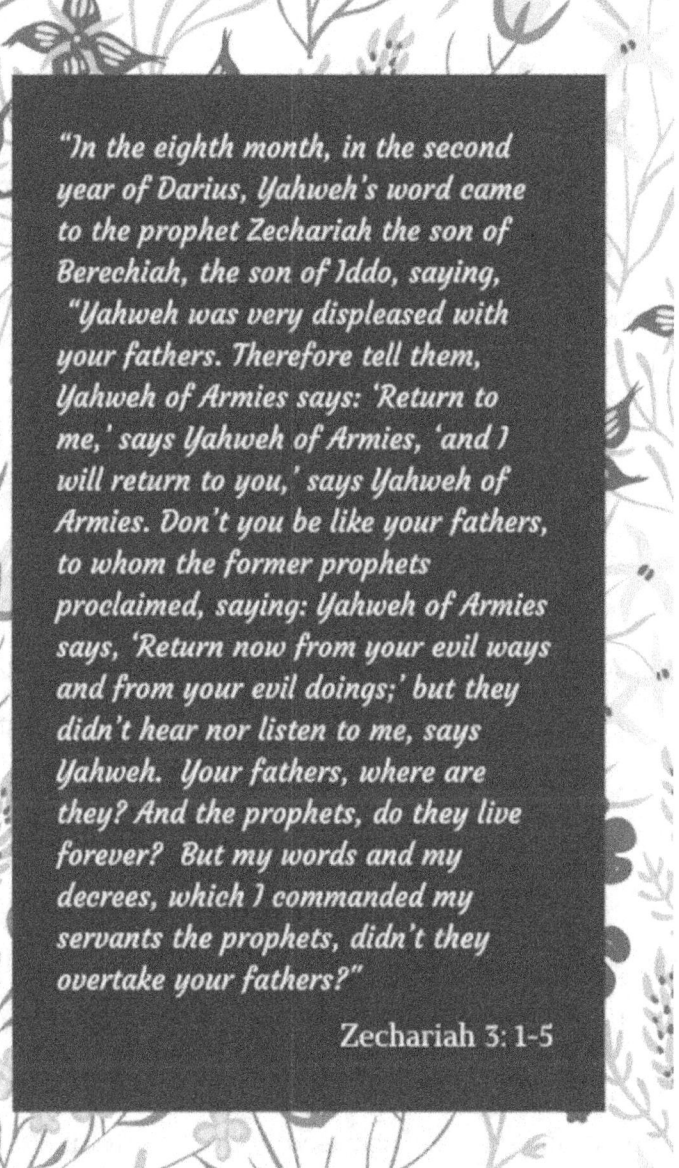

"In the eighth month, in the second year of Darius, Yahweh's word came to the prophet Zechariah the son of Berechiah, the son of Iddo, saying, "Yahweh was very displeased with your fathers. Therefore tell them, Yahweh of Armies says: 'Return to me,' says Yahweh of Armies, 'and I will return to you,' says Yahweh of Armies. Don't you be like your fathers, to whom the former prophets proclaimed, saying: Yahweh of Armies says, 'Return now from your evil ways and from your evil doings;' but they didn't hear nor listen to me, says Yahweh. Your fathers, where are they? And the prophets, do they live forever? But my words and my decrees, which I commanded my servants the prophets, didn't they overtake your fathers?"

Zechariah 3: 1-5

The angel of the LORD is Jesus, who gladdens our hearts.

The disciples rejoiced when they saw Jesus. The presence of the Lord is felt wherever His name is invoked. He does much for His people, even if we don't notice it.

We continue to have faith in Him!

The Scripture says that many will fail on the way and in the last few days the charity of many will cool down, but the word of the Lord, turning to His own, is: "He who is holy, let him be holy still" *(Rev. 22: 11)*

He is coming, and His return is much closer than you can imagine, and we want to ask Him to prepare us for that day. Our happiness is when, by the Spirit, we watch that face, and our joy is when we contemplate it.

The psalmist said, "Who is the man that you take care of him?" *(Psalm 8)*. He saw God's greatness and compared it with the smallness of man. In Revelation chap.19, it is written that the Spirit of the prophet has the testimony of Jesus. The prophet, the believer, presents Jesus and we have nothing to present of our own, but we have in our hearts what Jesus put in: His love.

The prophet Zechariah saw the High Priest Joshua standing upright in the presence of God, and he was in poor condition, in filthy clothes, but he persisted in wanting to remain in His presence.

The Lord knows our needs, and the more we realize how much He loves us and how many times He comes to our rescue, the more devoted we become to Him. The priest hoped and trusted in God's presence, although his condition was not adequate, because he was wearing filthy clothes. To the priest's right, however, was the enemy accusing him, to discourage him. How many times the enemy wants to discourage even our soul, but we must not be discouraged, and we must remember the Word of God: "If your mother and father forsake you too, I will never forsake you." (*Psalm 27:10*)

God's love is so deep that man cannot measure it, because God so loved

the world, to which gave His only begotten Son, that whosoever believeth in Him should not perish, but have eternal life. The Lord knew that Adam and Eve, for their disobedience, would find themselves in a desperate condition. They saw each other's nakedness and covered themselves with fig leaves, but they had to have a sad experience. When the sun came up, the leaves dried up and found themselves naked.

Unfortunately, they listened to the enemy, and gave in to flattery instead of the truth of the Lord. We must have more faith in the Lord! We need Jesus in our lives, not people, words and religions.

Let's do as Philip said to Nathanael: "It's useless to make multitudes of words; come and see". The Lord looked for Adam and Eve because they needed to be dressed.

Who knows how many of God's children are naked! It is written in the book of Revelation, chap. 3: "You who say that you are rich and need nothing more I will give you, I suggest you buy me some fire-hardened gold because you are that poor, blind man, and you're that naked."

May the Lord clothe our souls. We want to live under the holy robes that the Lord gives us by grace. God called Adam, but he hid and said, "Lord, when You called me into the garden, I have heard Your voice."

Many hear the voice of the Lord and hide.

Peter and John before the Consistory (tribunal) said: "...for as far as we are concerned, we cannot do, but speak the things that we have seen, and heard...", because on the mountain of the transfiguration they heard "This is my beloved son, hear Him". And the disciples answered: "Judge ye, if it is just in the sight of God, to obey you, rather than God".

Obedience is worth more than sacrifice.

Let's hold on to Jesus because one day, before the door of Heaven, we will not meet our friends, the relatives or acquaintances, but Jesus, who will put His hand on our shoulder and say, "Come in, the blessed of my Father, you who have done my will."

The Lord sought Adam and Eve to dress them.

He does not like to see us naked, or that we wear artificial clothes, or that we are dressed in a religion, but he wants us dressed in his armor.

The Lord, seeing the condition of Adam and Eve, took skins and covered them.

He wants to dress us too!

Who knows how many thorns we encountered on the way that tore our clothes off; who knows how many thorns. How many times, though looking to the Lord, does Satan come with his thorns to snatch from us the dress, but we want to ask the Lord to dress us for His Holiness and carry us forward for His glory.

Innocent animals were killed to clothe Adam and Eve; to clothe us there was no need of animals, but Jesus, the Lamb of God, was crucified, and through that vermilion and the precious blood that has been poured out for us, the Lord has whitewashed our robe and has given us purity.

John in Revelation saw the saints dressed in white.

Only the blood of the Son of God can cleanse us from our sins. The priest had dirty clothes, but he waited for everything by grace. Blessed are we if we wait for everything from the Lord, and blessed are we if we're entitled to God's presence. When we don't feel His presence, we go looking for Him because He enriches our lives. God said to Abraham, "Walk before me and be close to me". He delights when we walk with Him.

The enemy, accusing Joshua, said: "You are clothed in dirty clothes; how can you stay in the presence of the Lord? You'd better leave and come another time; maybe in more decent clothes." How many times the enemy puts so many obstacles in front of us, such as feeling unwell, or so busy that we don't show up for the appointment with the Lord. We often forget that we need Jesus more than we can imagine because when we stand before Him we receive new strength, fresh anointing, and He lifts our minds to heaven, and we enter into a heavenly atmosphere. The enemy accused the priest, but from the Throne began the voice that said, "Thou shalt rebuke the LORD, O Satan," and added that it was He who chose Jerusalem.

It is from the throne that we receive revelation!

Who knows how many ropes and how many chains He breaks when we stand before Him, that we may enter in the freedom of the Holy Spirit, and we move free on the path of holiness.

The enemy knows this is the end for him.

The day the angels sang hymns to God and the glory of the Lord went up and down from heaven, Satan trembled, but on the same day, our hearts were filled with joy. He who came breaks the chains of the devil. He who puts man in the full freedom of the Spirit so that he may understand the Lord's love. When Jesus was crucified he raised his eyes to heaven saying, "Father, all is accomplished," Satan's head was crushed. He won and we also we will win if we walk in his footsteps.

Joshua's perseverance was rewarded.

The Lord, after having scolded Satan, said, "Take these clothes off Joshua. The Lord also wants to do something in us, His hands take away the garments that are not suitable for us. We do not want to be disobedient like the one who entered the wedding without having the suitable dress. The priest was stripped of those filthy robes, which were there because the man came from the great tribulation, and the Lord said so when He said that he was an ember escaped from the fire. We need be clothed in the Spirit, to take the full armor of Christ if we want to enter the fight and emerge victoriously. One of the enemy's pitfalls is to get us to the fight with our own forces, but let us do as David said to the giant Goliath: "I come to you not in my name but in the name of the Lord God of hosts, whom you have outraged." And in that name, the giant's head was cut off.

The Lord has given us victory over the devil and we must be faithful to Him. The enemy knows his end is near and he walks like a roaring lion, he knows his days are numbered and therefore he launches fire everywhere, but the Lord sees this.

He also looked upon the devil when the children of GOD were presented to him, and the enemy stood over him next door.

Even on that occasion, the Lord scolded the enemy, saying, "What are you looking for? Have you set eyes on my servant Job?" The Lord has also given Job victory.

After Adam and Eve disobeyed the Lord by eating the fruit that had been forbidden him to eat, the Lord said, "You are dust." He condemned them, but thanks be to God that Jesus gave us victory. Job said, "I know that my Redeemer lives and that He will take me from the dust".

Jesus came to take us out of the dust and take us to heaven.

The Lord's work continued in the priest Joshua, He took a tiara and placed it on his head.

Joshua needed to receive this. We too need to receive the mind of Christ!

May the Lord touch our minds so that we may stand still and walk together with Jesus.

The enemy was scolded, the priest was clothed in new garments, and the glory in the end, was of the Lord.

Our victory will be like this when we go with the Lord to reign for all eternity.

CHAPTER 14 - GUIDE FOR THE BLIND

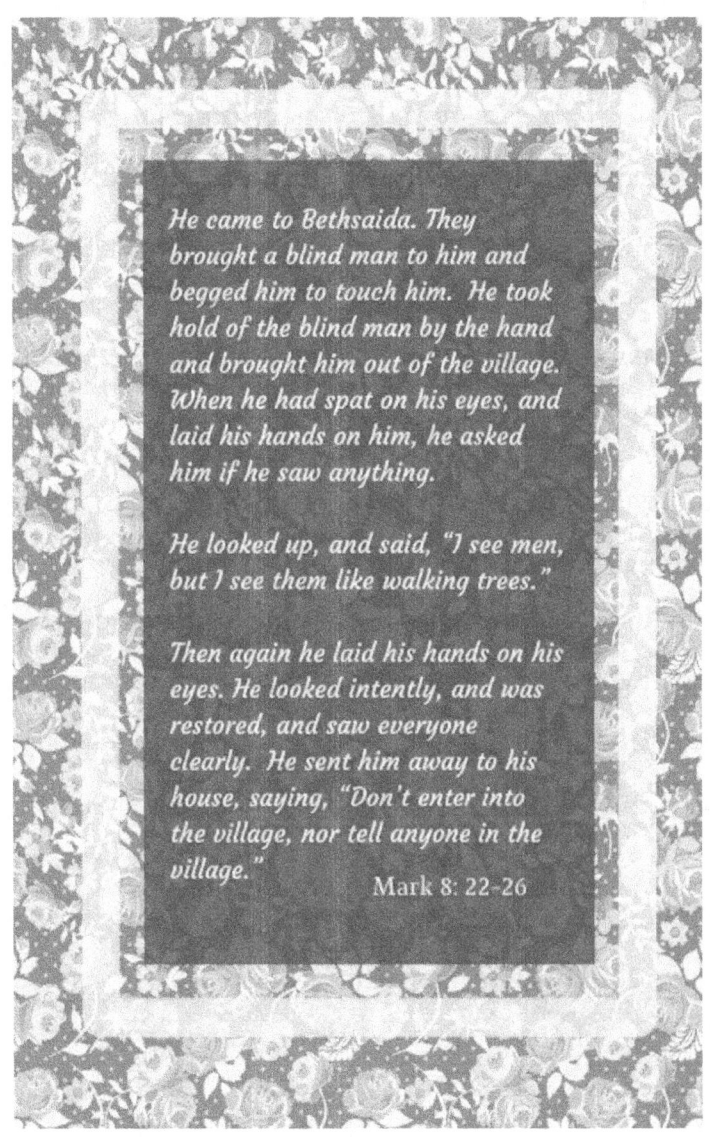

He came to Bethsaida. They brought a blind man to him and begged him to touch him. He took hold of the blind man by the hand and brought him out of the village. When he had spat on his eyes, and laid his hands on him, he asked him if he saw anything.

He looked up, and said, "I see men, but I see them like walking trees."

Then again he laid his hands on his eyes. He looked intently, and was restored, and saw everyone clearly. He sent him away to his house, saying, "Don't enter into the village, nor tell anyone in the village."

Mark 8: 22-26

The Lord leads the blind people by a path they do not know.

He wants to lead us and carry us forward for His glory. In the scripture, there are many blind people: Bartimaeus is one of them, who sat in the street asking alms, but when she heard that Jesus was passing through Jericho, he didn't stay in the same one condition, but he began to praise the Lord aloud, saying things that others did not know, but which the Spirit revealed to him.

And the blind man called Jesus *son of David*, that is *the son of kings*. There are many people, even today, who, although following Jesus, do not know the reality of the Spirit, and they do not know the true teaching of heaven, the true faith, and the true anointing; but the true servant of God is called to walk under the anointing of heaven. That costs money, and it's not easy! Jesus said that we have to give up on ourselves, and that's very difficult, because it's just when it feels like we're there.

We suddenly take something of our own and leave the Lord's. The blind man of Jericho then received a great revelation; the same one that the nailed man received on the cross next to Jesus who, rebuking his companion, said: "We truly we deserve this punishment, but He, Jesus, did nothing". But as he said this, the other insulted Jesus, and the first one said: "You don't even fear God". Many people are not afraid of the Lord, even if they look like little dogs walking in silence. But one day, when He returns, everything will be brought to light and all that was hidden will be revealed. When Bartimaeus was called by the Lord he immediately left the cloak that had on him, because he knew that when the Lord calls, he wants to operate in the life of the person. We too have been called by the Lord and therefore we must let Him work in our life. Bartimaeus did not only receive his sight but, as the scriptures say, he followed Jesus. He changed at any moment. But some people have known the Lord for years and remain the same, while those who have truly put their lives in the hands of the King will follow him. There is another blind man in the scripture, the born blind, who was so that he would manifest the glory of God.

God uses various methods to work each soul, depending on the character of the person.

All who love Him are to become humble and meek as Jesus was.

The born blind man was different from the blind man Bartimaeus. Jesus made a poultice and put it on his eyes, then told him to wash up in Siloe's pool, so his recovery depended upon obedience to the command of Jesus. And it was precisely because of his obedience that the blind man was healed and he received his sight. For this same obedience, later on, he was even thrown out of the synagogue, but yet he testified of Jesus, saying, "One thing I know is that before, I was blind, but now, I know I see."

He didn't care what the accusers told him, because he had entered a *new walk*, the one of light. When he was thrown out of the synagogue Jesus found him and revealed himself as the Son of God. Even the Apostle Paul, stopped on the road to Damascus, was blinded by a great light from heaven and he too had to be visited by God's grace. Ananias under the command of the Lord went to Paul, to whom, as the scripture says, some scales fell from his eyes. After what the Lord did to him, the Apostle Paul later said: "I consider mine wisdom dung before the excellence, knowledge of the Lord".

CHAPTER 15 - THE CHURCH DESTINED FOR THE KINGDOM

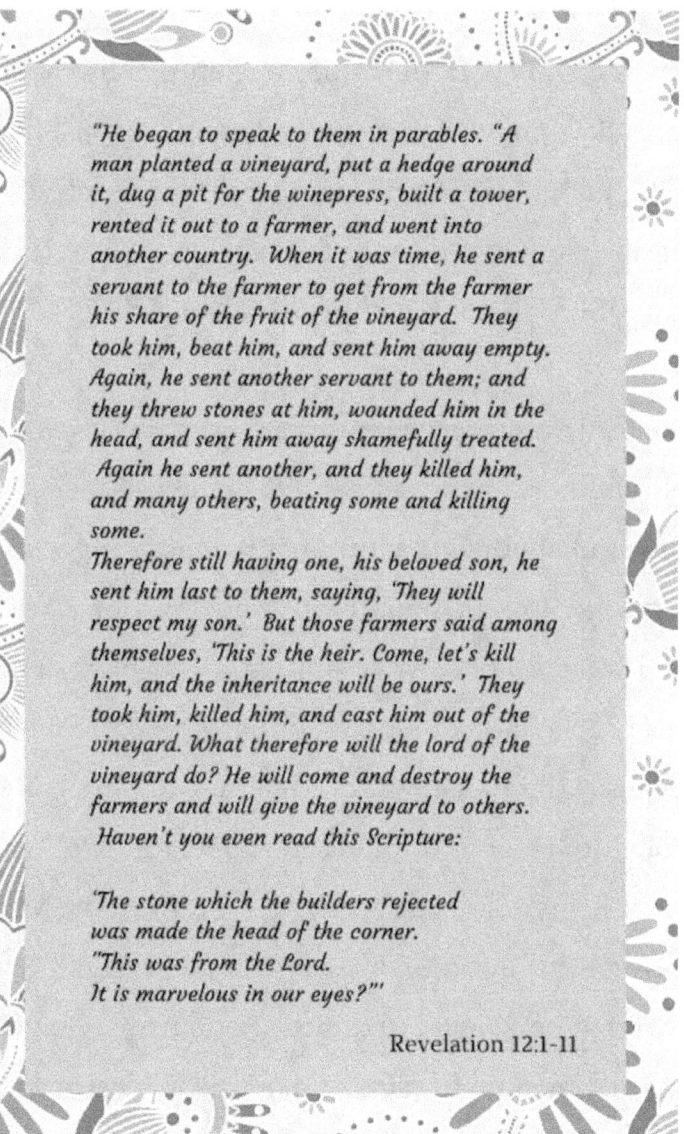

"He began to speak to them in parables. "A man planted a vineyard, put a hedge around it, dug a pit for the winepress, built a tower, rented it out to a farmer, and went into another country. When it was time, he sent a servant to the farmer to get from the farmer his share of the fruit of the vineyard. They took him, beat him, and sent him away empty. Again, he sent another servant to them; and they threw stones at him, wounded him in the head, and sent him away shamefully treated. Again he sent another, and they killed him, and many others, beating some and killing some.
Therefore still having one, his beloved son, he sent him last to them, saying, 'They will respect my son.' But those farmers said among themselves, 'This is the heir. Come, let's kill him, and the inheritance will be ours.' They took him, killed him, and cast him out of the vineyard. What therefore will the lord of the vineyard do? He will come and destroy the farmers and will give the vineyard to others. Haven't you even read this Scripture:

'The stone which the builders rejected
was made the head of the corner.
"This was from the Lord.
It is marvelous in our eyes?'"

Revelation 12:1-11

May God with His Word speak openly to our hearts!

The Lord doesn't just want us to go from territory to territory, from stature to stature, but He also wants that we walk from revelation to revelation; we must never stop.

In the path of the Christian, there must be no stops; at the limit of, the slowdowns, but never any stop! The Lord said to Abraham, "Shall I conceal from Abraham what I am about to do?"

The Lord wants to communicate, to speak as a father does with his children, He loves us with immense love. Sometimes we try to read about God's love, but the most important thing is to realize this love in our lives. But why don't we seek the revelation of the Lord? Why are we much more interested in religious propaganda or judging our brother? Are we interested in what Jesus, by grace, wants to tell us, teach us, and reveal? Let us pray to the Lord to put us in His school! We don't have to stay out of it anymore, but we have to get from the Master, who must always be in front of everyone. The Lord revealed to Abraham that he wanted to destroy Sodom and Gomorrah, and told him that by now the sins of those people had come to Him. It was then, that man began to understand the mysteries, and the revelations of God. We too are called to all this, to life of the Spirit, not to the existence of human culture. The Lord delights when we open our hearts to receive from Him.

When God created Adam dabbled, he spoke with his creature, even entrusted him with the task of choosing the names of all the animals. He put everything at his disposal, recommending them with love; only forbidden from eating the fruit of knowledge, that it may not end in death. God spoke, *He communicated clearly*.

Even today He still wants to speak to His Church!

When man disobeyed, he went into hiding, missing the appointment with God, which he did not used to miss.

The Lord sought him, but Adam did not want God to speak to his heart. If we let God speak in our life, we will become true disciples, true subjects of that glorious King, and true ambassadors of His Kingdom.

But now we enter into the message that the Lord, by grace, has given us.

To many people, it seems that the book of Revelation is, in many ways, incomprehensible, but the Lord wants us to enter into the Spirit, and into the apocalyptic territory; he wants us to begin to see Jesus in the majesty of His glory.

After passing through the gospels, one comes to see Jesus in glory; that is to say, a continuous growth spiritually. John was prepared, said he was in the Spirit and saw, as well as heard Jesus. At the same time, he listened to the messages given to the churches. Later he saw a very powerful ministry which is that of the measure of men, the worshippers and the altar. He continued until he was prepared to see: he saw a pregnant woman, bathed by the sun and at her feet was the moon. He saw the Church, the elect, the called by Christ; those to whom Jesus said, "It is not you who have chosen Me, but I who has chosen you."

He wants us to be a Royal Priesthood; he wants us to become vessels in honor of His glory.

While the woman is filled with the sun; Jesus, at her feet, is the moon.

We know that the moon reflects the light of the sun because it receives such light. Jesus said: "I am the light of the world." May God make us many luminaries for His glory!

Jesus also said that whoever has a lamp should not place it under a bushel, but where he can give it light.

If we have received grace, forgiveness, the call of heaven, and the baptism of the Holy Spirit, we present this great light, which has come to fill our lives, to those who still live in the darkness. The woman had a crown of twelve stars on her head, which means that she had entered the true apostolic ministry. There is no more room for our mind; our head must be crowned by that ministry. Like the Lord, the disciples also carried the message of salvation, but then they brought a new message, to bring the people to another vision, and to more territory. In the Acts of the Apostles, He said: "*...exhorting them to continue in the faith, and that through many afflictions we must enter into God's Kingdom*"[1] because the Church is destined for the Kingdom.

The woman who saw John was suffering from barrenness and she was troubled, which means that we do not enter in words, but with action, and present only the characteristics of the sky.

Let us remember that the slave who asked the master to allow him to be his slave in perpetuity, had the characteristics: his ear was pierced. When someone called him to service, he presented the ear as proof of belonging to another.

We belong to Jesus, as it is written in Psalm 50: "*Gather my saints together to me, those who have made a covenant with me by sacrifice*". The Lord did not choose men who sanctified themselves but sought out those who would make a pact with Him, and are willing to suffer, to be misunderstood, and to be hunted. The Lord summons these saints. John also saw the dragon with seven heads and ten horns, which is the height of being cunning. With his tail he carried away the third part of the stars in the sky.

---

[1] Acts 14:22

We know, from the same book, that the stars are the Angels of the church, and its messengers that could be us as long as we live a life consecrated to the Lord, high up in heaven, just like I'm the stars. When they are on high, they give light and guide, like the wise men... when they were directed in the search for Jesus, not man. The dragon does not do the greatest damage when it is in front of the person, but when it seems to be that it's going away: with its tail, it takes away the third part of the stars and throws it to the ground.

The scripture says that many people have started the work for the Spirit, but have perfected in the flesh! It could not drag the woman with it, so it stood before her and waited for her to give birth. It was not enough for him to have taken the third part of the stars with him, but he also wanted to take the male child. But at the moment of birth, the Lord intervenes to take the newborn male with him, and takes him safely to His Throne.

Let us take the Shulammite, who said that the garden she had was not her own, but belonged to another, to the Lord: "Go down into Thy garden."

May God grant us the strength so that we too may renounce ourselves and put everything into His hands! "...*Let my beloved come into his garden, and taste his precious fruits.*" [2]

---

[2] Song of Salomon 4: 16

Another example we have with the woman who filled the jars of oil; they didn't have to stay in front of her, otherwise, she might have been proud.

Even that male child did not remain before the woman but was taken to the Throne of God. The Lord said that if the vine branch stays tied to the vine, it will bear much fruit. As Shulammite said, only He is worthy to taste such fruits.

We must remain always in need before God, to be always ready to receive from Him, so that we are always empty of ourselves. The woman, as she was taken to the desert, did not worry about the male child, and went into the place prepared by the Lord, and there she was fed for one thousand two hundred and sixty days. Therefore, the *male child* must not remain in front of the woman, that is, *the fruit* of the church must not remain before it, but must be offered to the Throne of God.

The Lord also prepared the place for *Elijah*, who was given food and drink. The greatest ministers were prepared by the Lord in the desert. We know that *Moses* was prepared for the greatest minister in the desert to be the leader of the people of Israel and to free them from the slavery of Pharaoh. *Paul* was also prepared in the desert of Arabia and while the others had forgotten him, the Lord used Barnabas to help him. Therefore, the Lord provides for us to feed and console us also in the darker, more difficult times.

When Paolo and Sila were in prison there was no need for any earthly lawyer, but the heavenly lawyer was enough.

The writing goes on to say that there is a fight in the sky. This battle began, for each of us, on the day the Lord called us; for it is written that our battle is not against flesh and blood but against evil spirits. But He vanquished the dragon and his angels by throwing them to the ground. Then came the cry of joy and celebration, for not only the Lord won, but also those who were with Him. They won through the blood of the Lamb and never left that vision. The Lord's task is not to leave us in ignorance. The more we acquire the vision of God, the clearer will be the cunning and machinations of the enemy. The latter, however, is faced and overcome by the Lord.

We must no longer remain in the same methods, in the same stature, but we must walk with the revelation of the Lord.

What He does not reveal to us today, He will gracefully tell us tomorrow... But we must also ask Him to enter into His fullness.

He revealed to the disciples that there were many rooms in His Father's house. The Church is destined to receive God's revelations. Let us remember that the battles we face day by day are because of the enemy. Let us not let it carry us with its tail on the ground; let us not live for religiosity or artificial cults.

The cult of saints is directed to the Lord!

To the church of the Galatians Paul said: "My little children, I give birth to you again". Because the law had been mixed with grace, they were about to be thrown to the ground with their tails by the enemy, but the Apostle told them that he would give birth to them again, so that Christ Jesus might be formed in them.

CHAPTER 16 - MEETING WITH THE KING

Philip found Nathanael, and said to him, "We have found him of whom Moses in the law and also the prophets, wrote: Jesus of Nazareth, the son of Joseph."
Nathanael said to him, "Can any good thing come out of Nazareth?"
Philip said to him, "Come and see."
Jesus saw Nathanael coming to him, and said about him, "Behold, an Israelite indeed, in whom is no deceit!"
Nathanael said to him, "How do you know me?"
Jesus answered him, "Before Philip called you when you were under the fig tree, I saw you."
Nathanael answered him, "Rabbi, you are the Son of God!
You are King of Israel!"

John 1: 45-49

And he wants to become our King for each of us as well!

The Apostle Paul wanted to lose everything so that he would know Jesus as his King. Maybe we have not lost everything so far, but let's pray to the Lord to take from us what does not belong to Him. God's work is glorious and hidden from the human eye. Our desire must be to place us under the work of heaven, to be worked by the Lord. The prophet Jeremiah had to see that the one who worked on the wheel had the hands for forming the clay: the Lord knows how to work our hearts; we always need the hands of the Lord who works our lives. Philip and Nathanael reasoned around the coming of the Lord, for there were sufferings, bitterness, problems, but they knew that with His coming, He would have put everything in its place. That still happens today.

The woman of Samaria was also waiting for the coming of the Messiah, and she told Jesus this without knowing that the one in front of her was the One whom she was waiting for.

When we are gathered together, we often don't realize that the One before us is the King of glory who awaits us with open arms to give rest, joy and love. All this cannot be given by man, despite his efforts. No one can give what Jesus gives, because the gifts of heaven are not comparable to earthly ones as they are for a time, while heavenly ones are eternal. When we're tired and downhearted, the enemy traps our minds to bring us down, but thank God we have Him who protects us and restores us.

Philip and Nathanael, before He came, made many arguments, but with His coming, Jesus declared and preached in the way that a man cannot do.

Even in our lives, man has reasoned for a long time until Jesus came. The true People of the Lord do not like to see and hear man, but Jesus. Sometimes, as we do fall or be caught by other things, even the Shulammite was carried by the sons of the mother in so festive that at first, she could not comprehend it, but they were not their father's. There are very often children who are the mother's, that is, carnal! She did not find the atmosphere of the sky that raised her Bridegroom, in that the souls wanted to see only Him, but is in a carnal atmosphere in which they could not live like those who have been called from heaven. We know that there is no communion between the carnal (that seeks only his glory) and the spiritual (who seeks Him to whom the glory belongs). When Philip introduced Jesus to Nathanael as the Messiah, he went a little further, pointing out the place of origin. These words created in Nathanael's heart a little resentment and he asked what good could come from a place as despised as Nazareth.

This teaches us that we must never point out the places, but only He who heals, saves and baptizes with the Holy Spirit.

All that remained for Philip was to bring Nathanael before Jesus so that he would realize who He was. We too are called to notice, to see the difference!

There was a time when there was a great apostasy in Israel and the prophet Elijah was commanded to go down to the stream: for his servants, the Lord always has places to welcome them, give them food and water. The Lord gave Elijah to drink with the water from the stream and gave him to eat through the crows. When Shulammite left her mother's children, the Lord did not perplex her, for she prayed to her Spouse that she might find favor with Him and the place where He feedeth the flock.

Men want to look for the places themselves, but the Lord's place is not the human place, but that of the Spirit; that is to say, the land where souls find pasture and they contemplate the presence of their Pastor.

John, in the Revelation, says he is in the Spirit in the place of the Lord on Sunday, that is in the Lord's Day. Only he who is transported into God's territory can see Jesus. The Lord said to the Shulammite: "...go out and follow the sheep trail." Jesus also said: "My sheep listen to my voice and follow me." The sheep of the Lord cannot follow the voices of the mercenaries because the voice of the Good Shepherd resembles the sound of many waters; even John, as he heard it, said, "I turned to see the voice of the Lord."

It's wonderful to hear that voice, we must look for his voice too!

The proposals of the five foolish virgins were different from those of the five prudent virgins, who were only interested in the coming of the Bridegroom. We too must be prepared!

In the book of the prophet Amos, the Lord says, "Prepare, O Israel, for the encounter with thy God.[3]

Nathanael did not need the words of Philip, but rather to meet the Lord personally to see who he really was, and to experience His blessings, as the woman with a flow of blood experienced when by touching the hem of His garment, Jesus released His virtues.

If only by touching the hem of His garment there is healing and salvation, let us imagine what means to touch Jesus!

He said to Mary Magdalene: "*Don't hold me, for I haven't yet ascended to my Father*"[4]. We must touch Jesus on the throne to receive the blessings that give eternal life. The words of man can't convince anyone. In this time, we have to bring every person to His presence. The man must disappear to make room only for Jesus.

---

[3] Amos 4: 12
[4] John 20: 17

The two disciples on the road to Emmaus rejoiced in recognizing Jesus as He broke the bread, and with this cheerfulness, they found the strength to face the night and the tiredness in their legs. They immediately returned to Jerusalem to share with the others their gaiety.

Scripture speaks to us of Greeks who no longer wanted to see Jesus from afar, but wanted to know Him personally[5]. Even today many people still look at Him from afar, with the risk of putting other things in front of Him and lose the vision; but we are called to see Jesus up close, to touch Him, to stay at His feet, to hear His voice and contemplate Him.

Even Zacchaeus, on the sycamore tree, looked at Jesus from afar, but He did not pass him by, but *called him by name. **The Lord knew Zacchaeus as he knew Nathanael and as he knows each one of us, by our names!***

Jesus had Zacchaeus watch closely, as he did with Nathanael.

The time has also come for the Church of the Lord to contemplate the Lord closely... As in the royal courts, the queen sits next to the king, so does the Church sit next to her Bridegroom.

---

[5] John 12:20-21

Jesus called Nathanael by name and told him that he had already seen him under the fig tree. Finally, Nathanael had to admit that He was the Christ, His God, the King of Israel.

The Shulammite followed the sheep's tracks in the most difficult hour: there is an hour of fire, and that of noon, which sometimes frightens even those who want to sanctify themselves to the Lord.

Today there is an hour of great religious enthusiasm, but in the hour so red-hot, He shows us where to pasture His flock, which is restored and quenched.

CHAPTER 17 - THE MEETING AT THE SEA OF TIBERIAS
(in-depth study)

> After these things, Jesus revealed himself again to the disciples at the sea of Tiberias. He revealed himself this way. Simon Peter, Thomas called Didymus, Nathanael of Cana in Galilee, and the sons of Zebedee and two others of his disciples were together. Simon Peter said to them, "I'm going fishing."
> They told him, "We are also coming with you."
> They immediately went out and entered into the boat. That night, they caught nothing. But when the day had already come, Jesus stood on the beach; yet the disciples didn't know that it was Jesus. Jesus, therefore, said to them, "Children, have you anything to eat?"
> They answered him, "No."
> He said to them, "Cast the net on the right side of the boat, and you will find some."
> They cast it, therefore, and now they weren't able to draw it in for the multitude of fish. That disciple therefore whom Jesus loved said to Peter, "It's the Lord!"
> So when Simon Peter heard that it was the Lord, he wrapped his coat around himself (for he was naked), and threw himself into the sea. But the other disciples came in the little boat (for they were not far from the land, but about two hundred cubits away), dragging the net full of fish. So when they got out on the land, they saw a fire of coals there, with fish and bread laid on it.
>
> John 21: 1-9

We want to ask the Lord to bring us to that apocalyptic stature where it is said: "...*and his servants will serve him. They will see his face, and his name will be on their foreheads*"[6]

It is very difficult to serve the Lord!

We often want to serve Him in our comfort and according to our thoughts, but one must enter into true service, into what emanates from the Lord a scent of holiness. We must be obedient in all ways; we must ask the Lord for the necessary forces to be able to walk behind Jesus without ever letting him out of your sight. Many people turned their eyes away from Jesus, but Peter, John and James who climbed the mountain of the Transfiguration never turned their eyes away from Him.

Jesus is our life, our joy, and rivers of living water flow from Him. It is the Lord who quenches our thirst. our souls and refresh our lives. The touch of Jesus' hand takes us into the heavenly spheres and makes us understand that we are strangers and pilgrims of this world. Jesus opens the gates of

---

[6] Rev. 22: 3,4

heaven to us. There are many doors in this world, but heaven hath only one: Jesus Christ, the Son of God.

He said that anyone who does not enter through Him is a thief, but we want to ask, every day more and more, to be sanctified in His word. Let us remember, however, that it is very easy to speak; even the Apostle Peter, when Jesus began to speak of the sufferings, saying that many were scandalized by Him, was immediate in saying: "Lord, even if all will leave you, I will not leave you". The Lord replied to him, looking at him with love: "Before the cock crows, you will have denied me three times"[7]

Previously, even the disciples said with ease: "Lord, we have left everything to follow you;"[8] it was true, but after they saw Jesus crucified, they returned to their old ways. They had understood little, or almost nothing, of Jesus.

There are many people still, who did not understand Jesus, but the Lord gives grace to every soul to understand Him.

The Holy Spirit told Simeon that he would not see death if he had not first seen Jesus. So, there was something else this

---

[7] Luke 22: 59
[8] Matt. 19: 27

wise old man needed: to see Jesus. We too we need to see Jesus, because that is how we are fortified in Him, consoled, blessed and we're safe from the enemy's pitfalls. But when we don't want to see Him, we are exposed to every temptation. Jesus prayed for Peter after he had denied Him[9]. Let's be grateful to God, He intercedes for us and comes to our aid. The disciples, believing that they had lost Jesus, returned to the sea and the boat, but the scripture tells us that, despite their efforts, they took nothing that night. One does not live for things artificial, but of things real, which have substance, and that can give us only the son of God. The Lord knew what the disciples needed; they wanted Him, His help, His love and His word. We need Jesus too, and He knows it.

Without Jesus we cannot go on, and we cannot understand the mysteries of God's Kingdom.

Jesus said: "*To you it is given to know the mysteries of the Kingdom of Heaven*"[10].

He loves us immensely and wants the torch of His love to be alive. Jesus presented Himself to the disciples in a glorious

---

[9] Luke 22: 32
[10] Matt. 13:11

way; he came quietly to the shores of the sea of Tiberias, looked at them as only Jesus can look, and began to speak to them.

He also looks into our hearts!

How many times we live dark hours but He wants every person to repent and receive the crown of Eternal Life. Jesus said he came on earth to save and to seek what was lost. He also sought us with love and with such kindness.

But when Jesus went to His own, they did not recognize Him. Many people can't even comprehend the presence of the Lord. When He comes, He wants to operate, put something new into our lives, anoint us, and enrich us. He comes to overwhelm us with His grace, and for that, we want to thank Him.

Jesus can talk to the tired man!

How many tired people have gone left and right without finding happiness, but let us remember that Jesus wants to show Himself to us, He wants to fill our nets and we must not be perplexed. It takes the grace of God to enrich our hearts.

Beware, however, because we could also have our granaries full of human thoughts, like the man who, thinking of the future, said, "I will unpack my granaries and make them bigger so that I may fill them"[11]. But the Lord does not want us to be full of things of this world.

When that man's work is done, it will have taken him time and money, but what he has done will not be of the heavenly root. It's written: "Blessed are all those who hope in things that belong to the Lord."[12] It was not so for this man, whose hope was for the things of this earth. The Lord called him foolish and said that night he would have to account for his soul. The scripture says that in vain do the builders toil, if it is not He who builds[13]. Who knows how many times we'd like to make something of ourselves, but salvation belongs to the Lord.

When the Apostle Paul was a prisoner in Rome, the Lord sent souls to him so that they would hear from his mouth, the anointed by the Holy Spirit, the message of Heaven. This message bore fruit in many hearts. The word of the Lord bears much fruit and we want to make it get into our hearts.

Jesus asked His disciples if they had caught any fish, but they said no; with His voice full of grace, Jesus said, "Cast the net on the right side of the boat, and you will find some."[14]

---

[11] Luke 12:19
[12] Jer. 17:7
[13] Ps. 127: 1
[14] John 21: 6

Disciples were accustomed to obeying that voice, and when they touched the net, they saw that it was full of fishes. The net must be cast into the Kingdom of the Spirit at the command of Jesus.

He, after having made a poultice over his eyes, told the born blind man to go and wash his eyes in Siloe's pool. The blind man obeyed the command and immediately afterward he began to see. We also want to obey the command of the Lord.

When they saw the net full of fish, the disciples noticed that only one person could do that action: Jesus.

How many times have we hesitated!?

Joshua called the people to come before God and said, "Choose today whom you will serve"[15]. We also serve Jesus because He comes to our aid and illuminates the dark moments of our lives. As for the three who went into the burning fiery furnace[16], they all thought that they would burn to death, but it was not so because the fire burned the bonds they had in their hands, and when the king looked out the window of the furnace, he saw that there was another person with those three: the Son of God. The world must find that among us there is the

---

[15] Josh. 24: 15
[16] Dan. 3: 11

living God, that we have the anointing and the power of the Holy Spirit. Even king Darius, when he had Daniel thrown into the lion's den, thought that he would be mauled, but he had to recognize Daniel as a servant of God when he cried out of the pit with joy: " My God has sent his angel, and has shut the lions' mouths, and they have not hurt me."[17]

The disciples also had to observe that Jesus was there to help them. Among them there was one who understood Jesus more: John, who, seeing the net full of fish, said, "It's the Lord."[18] Many times we go before Him regretful and full of problems, but He drives everything away.

Let's see that we have the Lord before us.

He said to Abraham: "Walk before Me and be blameless"[19]. We too must always be in His presence. When Peter realized that Jesus was standing in front of him, he immediately cinched his shirt and threw himself into the sea to reach the shore where Jesus was, while the others arrived by boat. Jesus had made the disciples fan the embers already lit and the fish roasting, but they also found the bread.

---

[17] Dan. 6: 21
[18] John 21: 7
[19] Gen. 17: 1

We too need to be fed with that bread, the Bread of Life!

Just as the Lord made the disciples find the food ready, so He prepares it for us again before bringing us into His presence, and we do nothing. Let us not strive for food which has no value, but let's do it for the one who has eternal life, leaving all that is not belonging to the Lord.

Elijah, after having drunk the water and eaten the cake that the Lord prepared for him, had to walk for a long time before he can reach God's mountain. Who knows for how long we too have wandered the sea of our thoughts without ever taking anything; but the Lord wants us to enter into the reality of the Spirit and make us walk with the vision of Jesus. He gave food to the disciples, and they were pleased; we too must be glad to see Jesus in front of us, we must be certain that He will not leave us and will never leave us.

As Jesus went to meet the disciples, He will always come to our rescue until the end.

We, too, must ask the Lord to fill the net for us, for we cannot walk with the empty heart.

Many people look like clouds, but the word of God tells us, however, that they are clouds without water, and we want to ask the Lord to fill us with Him. The scripture also tells us of others who are like chaff driven by the wind; there are many winds of doctrine, but we just want to be close to Jesus. The disciples began to understand their shortcomings (we have some too), but God intervenes in this too.

He loves us and wants us to become pillars of His temple.

He does not leave us; on the contrary, the Lord says: "It will happen that your mother and father will leave you, but I will never abandon you" and then again: "It will happen that mothers will leave their children to feed, but I will not leave you, oh Jerusalem, because I have carved you in the palms of my hands".

The signs of the crucifixion speak among God's people; those nails, that ardent and divine love, that immaculate price that was paid for us, and that precious blood that was shed for us; it's all about the Lord's great love. Like Abraham, who said little and did much, we also want to be men of few words.

CONCLUSION

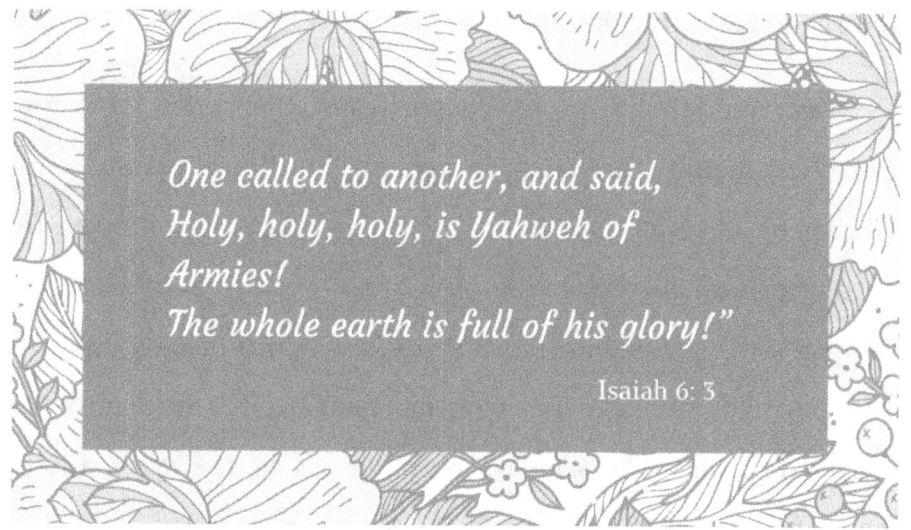

*One called to another, and said,
Holy, holy, holy, is Yahweh of
Armies!
The whole earth is full of his glory!"*

Isaiah 6: 3

The prophet Isaiah saw the Lord seated on a throne and saw how he was served by the Seraphim. They used their wings to hide rather than show their beauty. They jumped and glorified the Lord saying, "Holy, holy, holy is the LORD!"[20]

---

[20] Is. 6: 3

When Isaiah saw how the Lord was being served, he saw himself and realized that his lips were unclean, but God intervened and purified his lips.

Dear reader, the more we see Jesus, the better we know ourselves. Being Christians, in general, is different from being Christians of Jesus Christ. The Christian recognizes himself by speaking, because the true servant of the Lord lives by showing and presenting not himself, but Jesus. Isaiah not only had his lips purified, but also his spiritual hearing, for he heard the Lord say, "*Who shall I send? Who will go for us?*" He was ready to serve the Lord, so he answered: "*Here I am. Send me!*"[21]

Simon the Pharisee invited Jesus to his home but neglected Him. A woman came in, stood at Jesus' feet weeping, and with her tears, washed His feet, while with her hair, she dried them and kissed them. Then Jesus told the Pharisee that He had been invited into His house, but He had been neglected, and He had been offered nothing. We cannot neglect Jesus, He must be in the first place in our hearts. In difficult times, He comes to our aid and rescue. At the end of the book of Revelation 22:3, it is written: "*His servants will serve Him.*" We have for a time served more to ourselves than to the Lord, but the time will come when

---

[21] Is. 6: 8

we will serve Jesus with joy! Those who serve Him will see His face and have His name on their foreheads!

We are privileged; Jesus is watching over us.

www.ingramcontent.com/pod-product-compliance
Lightning Source LLC
Chambersburg PA
CBHW070941080526
44589CB00013B/1595